Applying for your ACR card – for foreigners in the Philippines

Arthur Crandon LL.B. (Hons.) M.A.

Applying for your ACR card – for foreigners in the Philippines

Copyright Arthur Crandon 2024

All rights reserved. No part of this book may be reproduced, stored in a retrieval system, or transmitted in any form or by any means—electronic, mechanical, photocopying, recording, or otherwise—without the prior written permission of the publisher, except for brief quotations in critical reviews or articles.

This is a work of fiction. Names, characters, places, and incidents are either the product of the author's imagination or used fictitiously. Any resemblance to actual persons, living or dead, events, or locales is entirely coincidental.

ISBN: 9798341467408

Cover design by Lynnie Ceniza
Interior design and formatting by Lynnie Ceniza
Published by Arthur Crandon Publishing
Visit our website: Arthurcrandon.co.uk

DISCLAIMER
The information provided in this book is for general informational purposes only. It does not constitute legal, financial, or professional advice. While every effort has been made to ensure accuracy, the author and publisher assume no responsibility for errors or omissions. Readers should consult with appropriate professionals for specific advice tailored to their individual circumstances.
First Edition: August 2024

The ACR card serves as an identification card for non-Filipino residents. It's issued by the Bureau of Immigration and contains essential information about the cardholder, including their visa status, length of stay, and other relevant details.

CONTENTS

	Acknowledgments	i
1	Requirements	1
2	Online Application	9
3	Change of Address	15
4	Other Online Services	23
5	Medical Records	31
6	E-Services	35
7	Technical Issues	39
8	Alternatives	43

The ACR card is not the only choice a foreigner has for how to stay in the Philippines long term – you should check out the alternatives in the last chapter

1 REQUIREMENTS

Let's delve into the details and requirements for obtaining an Alien Certificate of Registration (ACR) card in the Philippines. Whether you're a long-term resident, an expat, or a retiree, having an ACR card is essential for legal compliance and smoother transactions within the country.

What Is the ACR Card?

The ACR card, also known as the Alien Certificate of Registration I-Card, serves as an official identification card for non-Filipino residents. It's issued by the Bureau of Immigration and contains crucial information about the cardholder, including their visa status, length of stay, and other relevant details.

Requirements for Obtaining an ACR Card:

1. **Valid Passport with Visa:**
   - Your first requirement is a valid passport with an existing visa. Ensure that your visa is up-to-date and allows you to stay in the Philippines legally. If your visa is about to expire, consider renewing it before applying for the ACR card.

2. **Completed Application Form:**
   - Obtain the official ACR I-Card application form. You can usually find this form at the Bureau of Immigration office or download it from their website. Fill it out accurately and legibly.

3. **Proof of Address in the Philippines:**
   - You'll need to provide evidence of your local address. This could be a lease agreement, utility bill, or any official document that confirms your residence within the Philippines. Make sure the address matches the one you'll use on your ACR card.

4. **Payment of Fees:**
   - Prepare the necessary fees for the ACR card application. The fees typically include both a USD component (around $50.00) and a Philippine Peso (Php) component (usually around Php 500.00). Be ready to pay these fees during the application process.

5. **Passport Photos:**
   - Bring three recent and identical 2x2 photographs. These photos will be affixed to your ACR card. Make sure they meet the specified requirements (clear, well-lit, and with a white background).

Application Process:

1. **Visit the Bureau of Immigration Office:**
   - Locate the nearest Bureau of Immigration office. You'll need to apply in person. Check their operating hours and any specific requirements related to COVID-19 protocols.

2. **Submit Your Documents:**
   - Present your completed application form, valid passport, proof of address, and passport photos to the immigration officer. They will guide you through the process and verify your documents.

3. **Biometrics and Photo Capture:**
   - During your visit, you'll undergo biometric data collection (fingerprinting) and have your photo taken. These details will be used for your ACR card.

4. **Wait for Processing:**
   - Processing times vary, but you'll receive a claim stub with an estimated date for card issuance. Keep this safe and follow up as needed.

5. **Collect Your ACR Card:**
   - Return on the specified date to collect your ACR card. Bring the claim stub and any additional documents requested by the immigration office.

Additional Tips:

- **Renewal:** ACR cards have validity periods (usually one year or more). Renew your ACR card before it expires to maintain your legal status.

- **Change of Address:** If you move to a new address within the Philippines, update your ACR card promptly. Failure to do so may result in penalties.

- **Lost or Damaged Cards:** Report any lost or damaged ACR cards immediately. You'll need to apply for a replacement.

Remember, the ACR card is more than just a piece of plastic—it's your gateway to fully enjoying life in the Philippines!

How do I renew my ACR card?

Renewing your **Alien Certificate of Registration (ACR) card** in the Philippines is essential to maintain your legal status as a foreign national. Whether you're an expat, a retiree, or simply extending your stay, here's a step-by-step guide on how to successfully renew your ACR card:

1. **Complete Your Application:**

    o Obtain the appropriate ACR I-Card renewal application form. You can usually find this form at the Bureau of Immigration office or download it from their website. Make sure to fill it out accurately.
    o Attach all the required supporting documents as per the checklist. These documents typically include:
        - Your valid passport (with an existing visa).
        - Proof of your local address (such as a lease agreement or utility bill).
        - Recent passport-sized photos (usually three identical 2x2 photos with a white background).

2. **Visit the Designated Immigration Office:**
    o Locate the nearest Bureau of Immigration office. This is where you'll submit your application.
    o Present your completed application form along with the complete set of required documents. The immigration officer will guide you through the process.

3. **Biometrics and Photo Capture:**
   - During your visit, you'll undergo biometric data collection (fingerprinting) and have your photo taken. These details will be used for your renewed ACR card.

4. **Wait for Processing:**
   - Processing times vary, but you'll receive a claim stub with an estimated date for card issuance. Keep this safe and follow up as needed.

5. **Collect Your Renewed ACR Card:**
   - Return on the specified date to collect your renewed ACR card.
   - Bring the claim stub and any additional documents requested by the immigration office.

2 ONLINE APPLICATION

Renewing your **Alien Certificate of Registration (ACR) card** is essential to maintain your legal status as a foreign national in the Philippines. While the traditional process involves visiting the Bureau of Immigration office in person, there's good news: **online renewal** is now possible for certain categories of ACR cardholders!

Here's how you can go about it:

1. **Online Application (eServices):**

    o The Bureau of Immigration offers an **online application portal** called **eServices**[1]. You can use this platform for ACR I-Card

renewal if you meet the criteria.
- **Who can apply online?** All registered aliens and existing ACR I-Card holders (except Temporary Visitor's Visa holders or Tourist Visa holders) can use the eServices platform for renewal.

2. **Steps for Online Renewal:**
   - Visit the eServices portal.
   - Log in or create an account if you haven't already.
   - Look for the ACR I-Card renewal section.
   - Follow the instructions to submit your application online.
   - Make sure to attach any required documents (such as proof of address, passport photos, etc.).

3. **In-Person Renewal (Traditional Method):**
   - If you don't qualify for online renewal (e.g., if you're a tourist visa holder), you'll need to visit the nearest Bureau of Immigration office in person.
   - Bring your completed application form, valid passport, proof of address, and passport photos.

- Undergo biometric data collection (fingerprinting) and photo capture.
- Wait for processing and collect your renewed ACR card on the specified date.

4. **Cost:**
   - The cost for ACR I-Card renewal varies. Be prepared to pay the applicable fees during the process.

Remember, whether online or in person, renewing your ACR card ensures a smooth journey through the Philippine archipelago. So, keep those mangoes ripe and your ACR card up-to-date!

When renewing your **Alien Certificate of Registration (ACR) card** online in the Philippines, you'll need to gather the necessary documents to ensure a smooth process. Here's what you'll typically need:

1. **Completed Application Form:**
   - Fill out the ACR I-Card renewal application form accurately. You can usually find this form on the Bureau of Immigration's eServices portal.

2. **Photocopy of Passport Bio-Page:**
   - Make a photocopy of the bio-page of your valid passport. This page contains your personal information and photo.

3. **Photocopy of Current ACR I-Card:**
   - Provide a photocopy of your existing ACR I-Card. This card serves as proof of your legal status in the Philippines.

4. **Proof of Payment for Renewal Fee:**
   - Ensure you have evidence of payment for the renewal fee. This could be a receipt or confirmation of payment.

Remember that additional documents might be required based on your specific circumstances.

Correcting Errors

If you encounter an error in your **online ACR card application** in the Philippines, don't worry—I've got you covered! Let's address this hiccup and get you back on track:

1. **Review Your Application:**
   - First, double-check your application form. Ensure that all information is accurate and complete. Common errors include misspelled names, incorrect dates, or missing details. If you spot any mistakes, correct them promptly.

2. **Contact the Bureau of Immigration:**
   - If you've already submitted your application and notice an error afterward, reach out to the Bureau of Immigration. You can do this via email or phone. Explain the issue and ask for guidance on how to proceed.
   - They'll guide you on whether you need to submit a corrected application or if they can rectify the error on their end.

3. **Follow Up on Your Application:**
   - Regularly check the status of your application on the eServices portal. This helps ensure that your application is being processed.
   - If there's a delay or if your application encounters an issue,

you'll be aware and can take necessary action.

4. **Correcting Errors:**
   - If the error is minor (e.g., a typo), you may be able to correct it during the processing stage. However, if it's a significant error (such as incorrect visa details), you might need to submit a new application form with the correct information.

5. **Be Patient and Persistent:**
   - Mistakes happen, and immigration processes can be complex. Stay patient and persistent. The goal is to resolve the error and ensure your ACR card application proceeds smoothly.

Remember, even the most seasoned travelers encounter hiccups during paperwork. It's all part of the adventure!

3 CHANGE OF ADDRESS

If you need to **change your address** during the **renewal process** for your **Alien Certificate of Registration (ACR) card** in the Philippines, here's what you should do:

1. **Online Renewal (eServices):**
   - If you're eligible for online renewal (e.g., existing ACR I-card holders), log in to the eServices portal.
   - Look for the ACR I-Card renewal section.
   - Update your address information during the online application process. You'll likely find a field where you can input your new address.

2. **In-Person Renewal (Traditional Method):**
    - If you're renewing your ACR card in person, visit the nearest Bureau of Immigration office.
    - Bring the necessary documents for renewal (completed application form, valid passport, proof of address, etc.).
    - When submitting your application, inform the immigration officer that you need to change your address.
    - They will guide you on the next steps, which may include updating your address details.

3. **Required Documents for Address Change:**
    - To change your address, you might need to provide additional documents, such as:
        - **Certificate of Residence from the Barangay Captain:** This confirms your new address.
        - **Affidavit of Change of Address:** Prepare this document if required.
        - **Photocopy of your ACR I-**

Card: Include this as well.

4. **Be Thorough and Accurate:**
    - Ensure that the address change is accurately reflected in your application. Mistakes can cause delays or complications.

Remember, whether you're moving to a new island or just a few blocks away, keeping your ACR card updated ensures a smooth journey through the Philippine archipelago.

When renewing your **Alien Certificate of Registration (ACR) card** in the Philippines, you can also update certain personal details. Here's what you need to know:

1. **Change of Address:**
    - If you've moved to a new address within the Philippines, you can update it during the renewal process. Make sure to provide the necessary documents (such as a certificate of residence from the barangay captain) to support the address change.

2. **Name Changes:**
   - If your name has changed due to marriage, divorce, or any other reason, you can request an update. Prepare the relevant documents, such as a court order (if applicable), an amended/corrected birth certificate, and an affidavit of amendment of name or inclusion of name.

3. **Other Personal Details:**
   - While some changes (like marital status and name) are straightforward, others may require specific documentation. If you need to update any other personal details (such as gender, nationality, or occupation), consult with the Bureau of Immigration during your renewal process.

Remember, keeping your ACR card information accurate and up-to-date is crucial.

Using the eServices platform

Updating information through the **eServices platform** in the Philippines can vary depending on the specific context. Let's explore a couple of relevant scenarios:

1. **e-Travel Registration (Replacing e-Arrival CARD):**
    - Starting from December 1, 2022, the Philippine Government has transitioned from the old e-Arrival CARD Registration to a new **e-Travel Registration** system[1]. Here's what you need to know:

        - **Purpose:** The e-Travel Registration is mandatory for travelers arriving in the Philippines. It simplifies the arrival process and requires less information than the previous system.

        - **User-Friendly Interface:** The new platform offers a more user-friendly interface and will soon integrate with the requirements of Immigration and Customs authorities.

- **Filling Out the Form:** To avoid long lines at the airport, I highly recommend filling out the e-Travel Registration within 72 hours before departing from your country of origin. If you can't do it beforehand, personnel from the Philippine Bureau of Quarantine and airport staff will assist you upon your arrival in the Philippines.

- **Access the Portal:** You can access the e-Travel Registration portal at etravel.gov.ph.

2. **Bureau of Internal Revenue (BIR) eServices:**

    o The **Bureau of Internal Revenue (BIR)** also provides an eServices platform[2]. While this is primarily related to tax matters, it's worth mentioning:

- **Purpose:** The BIR eServices hub allows taxpayers to conveniently access updated information on Philippine tax laws, regulations, revenue issuances, and BIR programs and projects.

- **Accessibility:** Taxpayers can use this platform anytime, anywhere to stay informed and manage their tax-related matters.

Remember, whether you're updating travel information or tax-related details, these digital platforms aim to make processes smoother and more efficient.

4 OTHER ONLINE SERVICES AVAILABLE

The Philippines has been making strides in digital transformation, and several eServices are now available to streamline processes and enhance convenience for residents and visitors. Let's explore some of the key eServices:

1. **Bureau of Immigration eServices:**

   - The **Bureau of Immigration (BI)** offers an array of online services through its eServices platform[1]:
     - **Annual Report:** Registered aliens and ACR I-Card holders (except Temporary Visitor's Visa holders or Tourist Visa holders) can complete their annual report

online.

- **Emigration Clearance Certificate (ECC-B):** Departing holders of Immigrant and Non-Immigrant visas with valid ACR I-Cards can apply for ECC-B online.

- **Cruise Visa Waiver:** Visa-required nationals can apply for a cruise visa waiver online.

- **Special Study Permit:** Foreign nationals below 18 years old taking non-degree courses in the Philippines (less than 1 year) can apply online.

- **Petition for Re-acquisition / Retention of Philippine Citizenship:** Former Philippine citizens who have been naturalized in another country and wish to retain or re-acquire their Philippine citizenship can submit their application online.

- And more!

2. **Other eServices in the Philippines:**
    - Beyond immigration-related services, the Philippines offers various eServices across different sectors:

        - **e-Travel Registration:** This platform simplifies arrival procedures for travelers entering the Philippines. It replaces the old e-Arrival CARD system and allows travelers to submit necessary information online before their trip.

        - **BIR eServices:** The Bureau of Internal Revenue provides an eServices hub for taxpayers. It covers tax-related matters, including access to tax laws, regulations, and revenue issuances.

        - **Other Local Government Services:** These may include

online applications for housing, employment search, career development, voter registration, and more.

Remember, embracing eServices not only saves time but also contributes to a more efficient and connected society.

The Philippines has been making significant strides in digitalizing its healthcare services, and various eServices are now available to enhance convenience, accessibility, and efficiency. Let's explore some of the key eHealth initiatives and telehealth apps in the country:

1. **Teleconsultation Apps:**
    - **AIDE**: A teleconsultation app that connects patients with doctors and nurses from the comfort of their homes. Users can request checkups, and even emergency services like baby deliveries or care for the disabled and elderly.

    - **Medgate**: Offers telemedical consultations with affiliated doctors. After chatting with a telemedical assistant, patients are redirected to a physician who assesses their health status, provides e-prescriptions, and interprets lab results.

KonsultaMD: A telehealth membership service that provides 24/7 unlimited access to licensed doctors via voice or video calls. No appointment needed·

- **Kitika**: A subscription-based teleconsultation app that offers primary healthcare through video calls with nurses, general practitioners, and specialists. Users receive e-prescriptions and medicine delivery

-
    DockoTo: Developed by Ideahub, DockoTo connects users with medical specialists for online consultations anytime, anywhere.

2. **National eHealth Systems and Services**:
    - The Philippines aims to establish a National eHealth System and Services. This vision involves delivering health services through cost-effective and secure

information and communications technology (ICT).

3. **Digitalization in Healthcare**:
    - Digitalization initiatives include e-prescriptions, hospital management information systems, and electronic patient records[3].
    - The Integrated Clinic Information System (iClinicSys) is being implemented for primary care facilities.

4. **Benefits of eHealth**:

    - **Accessibility**: Telehealth programs link patients with healthcare practitioners across geographic boundaries, improving access to medical expertise.

    - **Efficiency**: E-prescriptions, online consultations, and digital health records streamline processes and reduce paperwork.

Remember, embracing eServices not only saves time but also contributes to a more efficient and connected healthcare system. Whether you're seeking medical advice or managing your health records, digital convenience awaits!

5 MEDICAL RECORDS

Accessing your medical records online in the Philippines has become more convenient due to digitalization efforts. Here are some ways to do it:
1. **St. Luke's Medical Center eHealth Patient Portal**:
    - If you're a patient at St. Luke's Medical Center, you can use their **eHealth Patient Portal**[1]. This portal allows you to:
        - View your medical records and patient information online.
        - Book ancillary procedures (such as lab tests or imaging) through the Order & Pay function.

- Request admission and select your preferred suite or private room—all within the portal.
2. **PhilHealth Member Data Record (MDR)**:
    - If you're a PhilHealth member, you can access your Member Data Record (MDR) online:
        - **PhilHealth Website**: Visit the PhilHealth website and create an account. Once registered, log in to your account, and you'll be able to view and print your MDR[23].
3. **Telehealth Apps**:
    - While not directly for accessing medical records, telehealth apps allow you to consult with healthcare professionals online. Some popular ones in the Philippines include:
        - **AIDE**: Connects patients with doctors and nurses for teleconsultations.
        - **Medgate**: Offers telemedical consultations and e-prescriptions.
        - **KonsultaMD**: Provides 24/7 access to licensed doctors via voice or video calls.
        - **Kitika**: Offers primary

healthcare consultations through video calls.
4. **Other Platforms**:
    - Check if your specific healthcare provider or hospital offers an online patient portal or eHealth services. Many institutions are gradually adopting digital solutions for medical records.

Remember to keep your personal information secure when accessing medical records online. Whether you're managing your health or seeking professional advice, these digital tools make healthcare more accessible and efficient!

6 E-SERVICES

Tell me more about eServices related to COVID-19 vaccination.
Copilot
Sent by Copilot:
Certainly! As part of the Philippines' efforts to manage COVID-19 vaccinations and facilitate safe travel, several eServices have been introduced. Let's explore some key platforms:
1. **VaxCertPH**:
    - **What Is It?** VaxCertPH is a digital vaccination certificate that fully vaccinated individuals can obtain online.
    - **Purpose:** It serves as proof of your full vaccination against COVID-19.
    - **Importance:** VaxCertPH is

especially relevant for travel, both domestically and internationally. It aligns with the International Certification of Vaccination (ICV), acting as a vaccine passport.
- **How to Obtain It:**
  - Visit the VaxCertPH website.
  - Agree to the privacy terms and conditions.
  - Provide your vaccination details (dates, doses, location).
  - Upload a copy of your valid ID and vaccination card.
  - Your certificate's validity is confirmed 14 days after registration[1].

2. **Common Vaccination Digital ID with QR Code**:
   - The Department of Information and Communications Technology (DICT) is working on a common vaccination digital ID for Filipinos. This ID will serve as proof of an individual's COVID-19 vaccination status.
   - Similar to the Excelsior Pass in other countries, this digital ID will likely include a QR code for verification[2].

3. **Availability for OFWs and International Travelers**:

- Initially, VaxCertPH was available to fully vaccinated international travelers and Overseas Filipino Workers (OFWs) in the National Capital Region (NCR). It's part of the DICT's Vaccine Information Management System (VIMS)[3].

Remember, these eServices contribute to safer travel and better pandemic management. Whether you're planning a trip or simply ensuring your health records are accessible, digital solutions are here to help!

7 TECHNICAL ISSUES

Encountering technical issues with vaccine certificates can be frustrating, but you're not alone! Let's tackle this together. Here's what you can do if you face any hiccups while dealing with your COVID-19 vaccination certificate:
1. **VaxCertPH Issues: Missing Records or Data Errors**:
    - Some individuals have reported missing records or errors in their personal data while applying for the VaxCertPH online. If you encounter this issue:
        - **Check Your Details**: Ensure that you've entered accurate information during the application process.
        - **Upload Supporting**

Documents: If your records are not found or contain errors, upload photos of your vaccination card and a government ID with a picture on the VaxCertPH website. These will be sent to the Department of Information and Communications Technology (DICT) for corrections.
- **Be Patient**: Corrections may take up to 24 hours, so give it some time[1].

2. **Incorrect Encoding by LGUs**:
   - Errors can occur due to incorrect encoding by local government unit (LGU) personnel. Here's what happens:
     - LGUs rely on the forms submitted to them, which are then encoded by their staff.
     - Sometimes, the quality of handwriting or clarity affects the encoding process.
     - If you notice incorrect details, contact the DICT to speed up the correction process[1].

3. **PhilHealth Member Data Record (MDR)**:
   - If you're a PhilHealth member, you

can access your Member Data Record (MDR) online. Visit the PhilHealth website and create an account. From there, you can view and print your MDR[2].

4. **Be Persistent and Seek Assistance**:
    - If you're still facing issues, don't hesitate to seek help. Contact the relevant authorities (such as the DICT or your local health office) for guidance.
    - Remember, technology can be quirky, but we'll get those certificates sorted out!

8 ALTERNATIVES

If you're a foreigner staying in the Philippines and looking for alternatives to the **Alien Certificate of Registration (ACR) card**, there are a few options to consider:

1. **Tourist Visa Extensions**:
    - If you're planning to stay in the Philippines for less than 59 days, you can extend your stay by applying for tourist visa extensions. These allow you to remain legally in the country without obtaining an ACR card. However, keep in mind that you'll need to renew your extension every two months.

2. **Special Resident Retiree's Visa (SRRV)**:
   - The SRRV is an option for retirees who want to live in the Philippines long-term. It requires a financial commitment (such as a deposit or investment) but provides more flexibility than a standard tourist visa. SRRV holders enjoy permanent residency status and can stay indefinitely.

3. **Permanent Resident Visa (13A Visa)**:
   - The 13A Visa is for foreign nationals married to Filipino citizens. If you're married to a Filipino, you can apply for this visa, which grants permanent residency. It eliminates the need for an ACR card and allows you to stay in the Philippines without time restrictions.

4. **Other Long-Term Visas**:
   - Depending on your circumstances (such as employment, business, or investment), explore other long-term visa options. These may include work visas, investor visas, or special non-immigrant visas.

Remember that each visa type has specific requirements, and it's essential to consult with the Philippine Bureau of Immigration or seek legal advice to choose the best option based on your situation. Whether you're enjoying retirement, working, or exploring the beautiful islands, there's a visa pathway that suits your needs!

ABOUT THE AUTHOR

Arthur Crandon is a retired lawyer and a prolific writer. He is British and grew up in a rural community in Somerset. He has lived in England, Wales, Hong Kong and the Philippines and now spends most of his time in the Philippines with his Visayan wife and their son.

He loves to hear from anyone who has anything to do with the Philippines – you can email him anytime on:

ac@arthurcrandon.co.uk

www.ingramcontent.com/pod-product-compliance
Lightning Source LLC
Chambersburg PA
CBHW070416230526
45471CB00006B/2841